Literacy Through Dramatic Play

Stories, Songs, and Rhymes with Reproducible Hats

Diane Dzamtovski

Illustrated by Bob Masheris

Rigby Best Teachers Press

An imprint of Rigby

Dedication: *To Mandred, Indred, and Sapphire - thanks for your guidance.*

Editor: Pam Gunter
Executive Editor: Georgine Cooper
Designer: Masheris Associates, Inc.
Design Production Manager: Tom Sjoerdsma
Cover Illustrator: Bob Masheris
Cover Photography: Sharon Hoogstraten
Interior Illustrator: Bob Masheris

07 06 05
10 9 8 7 6 5 4 3

Printed in the United States of America

ISBN 0-7398-7597-3
Literacy Through Dramatic Play

Table of Contents

Hats and Props

Fanciful reproducible hats and props

Introduction

Dramatic play is a powerful tool in the preK to second grade classroom. Through dramatic play, children try on different roles as they recreate and reenact a story.

Additionally, dramatic play helps children develop in many ways including:

- self-expression
- self-esteem
- imagination
- cooperation with peers
- responding to stories, songs, and rhymes
- expansion of oral language abilities
- problem-solving

How to Use This Book

The stories, songs, and rhymes selected for this book include simple plots and memorable characters from a variety of cultures. The selections may be used in any order.

Choose a story, song, or rhyme for the class; then read it all the way through to children a number of times so they become very familiar with it. When you read it again, you may want children to chime in during appropriate parts.

The reproducible hats and occasional props are furnished for you in this book. The props are to be in reproducible form to use as hats or cut out and used as hand-held props. However, the emphasis for dramatic play is on *process* rather than product. Therefore, no special equipment is really needed.

You can play the role of narrator, prompting children to say their lines or encouraging them to provide the action necessary to complete the story. Or you can work with children to develop a script based on the story, song, or rhyme before beginning the dramatic play.

As you assign roles, keep in mind that more than one child can play the same role simultaneously. For example, you could assign one child the role of the Itsy Bitsy Spider and repeat the song enough times so that all the children who want to play the role get a chance to do so. You can have many children playing Itsy Bitsy Spiders and reenact the song as a "chorus".

Of course, there is also the option to do both. For example, if the class is reenacting the story *The Bear and the Turtle*, you can have one child play the Bear, another child play the Turtle, and a group of children play the role of the Fox so that every child in the class has a role to play.

It is up to you and the interest and ability levels of children in your class.

Assign roles and reproduce hats and props as necessary. At the end of each story, song, or rhyme is a graphic key indicating the hats and props needed and the page or pages you can find them on. Some of the hats are used in more than one story. There are some suggestions for optional hats – hats not completely necessary to the story, song, or rhyme, but ones that you might want to include.

Some props can be used with more than one story, song, or rhyme. The spoon and the bowl can be "filled" by children with drawings that represent porridge for *Goldilocks and the Three Bears*, curds and whey for *Little Miss Muffet*, and yams for *Anansi and Turtle*.

Extending the Story, Song, or Rhyme

It is in extending the story, song, or rhyme that children can:

- work out problems and experiment with solutions
- pretend to be someone or something else
- take on another's perspective
- explore alternative situations
- explore issues of control
- communicate thoughts and feelings

Once children have reenacted the selection, encourage them to create their own sequels or "what if" plays. For example, ask children questions like the following and have them role-play based on those scenarios.

What might have happened if Goldilocks came back to visit the Three Bears again?

What might have happened if Anansi did share his meal with Turtle? How might the ending of the story change because of that decision?

Think about what if Goldilocks and Little Miss Muffet got together one afternoon. What would they talk about?

There are many options and opportunities for children to use their imaginations in a variety of ways.

After each story, song, or rhyme you will find the *Read to Me* icon Read to Me... with a letter to send home with the story just read. It asks for a caregiver to allow the child to retell the story and provides an opportunity for the child to act it out. This is added as an optional take-home extension. The take-home extension helps to provide caregivers with the stories that the children have read and promote the development of oral language and motor skills at the same time.

Assembling the Hats

1. Reproduce the necessary number of hats for the story, song, or rhyme you have selected.
2. Invite children to color the hats.
3. Cut out the pieces.
4. Align the graphic symbols and staple, glue, or tape the pieces together adjusting the hats to fit each child's head, as necessary.

An extender piece has been included on page 96 if you wish to make the hats larger.

The Bear and the Turtle

A Seneca Tale

One snowy day, Bear was taking a brisk walk through the woods. He was feeling quite proud of himself. When he saw Turtle at the edge of the lake, he said, “I am the fastest animal in the forest.”

Turtle heard him and said, “No, you’re not, Bear. I’m a lot faster than you.”

“How can that be?” said Bear. You are the slowest animal in the forest.”

“Well,” said Turtle. “Let’s have a race and we’ll see who is the fastest.”

“Okay,” said Bear.

They both agreed that Bear would run along the bank of the lake and Turtle would swim in the water. But the lake was frozen.

“I will make holes in the ice,” Turtle said. “Then when we start to race, I’ll put my head up and say something each time I come to a new hole.”

Bear agreed and the race was set for early the next day.

The next morning, many of the other animals came to watch. It was decided that Fox would give the signal for the race to start. He shouted, "Ready, set, go!" and off they went.

Bear started to run. Turtle's head disappeared under the first hole as she began to swim around the lake. In almost no time at all, Turtle's head came up at the second hole.

Turtle shouted, "Come on, Bear. Catch up to me!" And then Turtle's head disappeared again.

Bear was astonished that Turtle could swim so fast. Bear began to run even faster. But before he could get much farther, Bear saw Turtle's head pop up again.

Turtle shouted, "Come on, Bear. You can run faster than that. Catch up to me!"

And so it went. Bear ran and ran as fast as he could. He ran so fast that his legs began to hurt. But as fast as Bear ran, Turtle was ahead of him calling out to Bear to catch up.

When Bear reached the finish line, he was so tired he could hardly crawl. Turtle was already there, surrounded by Fox, Deer, and all the other animals. They were shouting, "Turtle won! Turtle won the race!"

Bear slowly walked home to his cave. He fell asleep as soon as he got there. He was so tired that he slept all the rest of the winter.

Meanwhile, Turtle waited at the lake until all the other animals went home. When Turtle was alone, she tapped on the ice. Suddenly, heads popped up through all the holes in the ice. It was Turtle's brothers and sisters and most of her cousins. And what do you know? They all looked just like her.

Turtle said, "I want to thank you all. Today we taught Bear a good lesson. And we have shown Fox and all the other animals that we are not the slowest animal in the forest."

Hats

Bear	page 60	Deer	page 63
Turtle	page 61	Horse	page 94
Fox	page 62		

Read to Me . . .

Today we read and acted out *The Bear and the Turtle*. Attached you will find a copy of the story that we read. Ask me to tell you about it. Then let's read it together while I act it out. Ask me questions about the story, like, *Who is my favorite character? Where do you think the story took place? How do you think the turtle won the race?*

Thank you for caring to read to me.

The Bear Went Over the Mountain

The bear went over the mountain,
The bear went over the mountain,
The bear went over the mountain,
To see what he could see.

To see what he could see,
To see what he could see,
The bear went over the mountain,
To see what he could see.

The other side of the mountain,
The other side of the mountain,
The other side of the mountain,
Was all that he could see.

Was all that he could see,
Was all that he could see,
The other side of the mountain,
Was all that he could see.

Hats

Bear page 60

Read to Me . . .

Today we read and acted out *The Bear Went Over the Mountain*. Attached you will find a copy of the song that we sang and read. Ask me to tell you about it. Then let's read it together while I act it out. Ask me questions about the song, like, *What do you think you would see on the other side of a mountain?*

Goldilocks and the Three Bears

Once upon a time there were three bears who lived in a house in the forest. There was a great big Papa Bear, a middle-sized Mama Bear, and a teeny tiny Baby Bear.

One day Mama Bear made some porridge but the porridge was too hot to eat. So the three bears decided to take a walk in the forest to let the porridge cool off. And off they went.

There was a little girl named Goldilocks and she, too, was walking in the forest. She was tired and hungry so she was very happy when she saw the three bears' house. She knocked on the door but no one answered, so she opened the door and walked in.

On the table in the kitchen were three bowls of porridge – a great big bowl, a middle-sized bowl, and a teeny tiny bowl. Goldilocks tasted the porridge from the great big bowl.

"This porridge is too hot," she said.

So she tasted the porridge from the middle-sized bowl.

"This porridge is too cold," she said.

Then she tasted the porridge
from the teeny tiny bowl.

"Ah, this porridge is just right!"
she said and ate it all up.

By now Goldilocks was feeling pretty tired. She saw three chairs in the living room – a great big chair, a middle-sized chair, and a teeny tiny chair. She sat down in the great big chair.

"This chair is too hard," she said.

So she sat down in the middle-sized chair.

"This chair is too soft," she said.

Then she sat down in the teeny tiny chair.

"Ah, this chair is just right!" she said. But just as she really got comfortable, the chair broke into pieces.

Now Goldilocks was very sleepy. She decided to take a nap and went upstairs to the bedroom. There she saw a great big bed, a middle-sized bed, and a teeny tiny bed.

She lay down on the great big bed but it was too hard. She lay down on the middle-sized bed but it was too soft. She lay down on the teeny tiny bed and it was just right. Goldilocks fell fast asleep.

Just then, the three bears came home from their walk in the forest. They came into the kitchen and looked at the three bowls of porridge.

“Someone has been eating my porridge,” said Papa Bear.

“Someone has been eating my porridge,” said Mama Bear.

“Someone has been eating my porridge and they ate it all up,” said Baby Bear.

The three bears went into the living room.

“Someone has been sitting in my chair,” said Papa Bear.

“Someone has been sitting in my chair,” said Mama Bear.

“Someone has been sitting in my chair and they’ve broken it all to pieces,” said Baby Bear.

The three bears went upstairs to the bedroom.

“Someone has been sleeping in my bed,” said Papa Bear.

“Someone has been sleeping in my bed,” said Mama Bear.

“Someone has been sleeping in my bed and she’s still there,” said Baby Bear.

Just then, Goldilocks opened her eyes and saw the three bears staring down at her. She jumped out of the bed and ran down the stairs. She quickly opened the kitchen door and ran away into the forest.

The three bears never saw Goldilocks again.

Hats

Golidlocks page 64
Papa Bear page 65
Momma Bear page 66
Baby Bear page 67

Props

Spoon and Bowl–"filled" with porridge page 68

Read to Me . . .

Today we read and acted out *Goldilocks and The Three Bears.* Attached you will find a copy of the story that we read and props that we used. Ask me to tell you about it. Then let's read it together while I act it out. Ask me questions about the story, like, *Who is my favorite character? Where do you think the story took place?*

Thank you for caring to read to me.

Little Bear, Little Bear

A Spanish Counting Rhyme

Little Bear, Little Bear can you jump?
Yes, yes, help me, help me count.
One, two, three, four, five, six,
seven, eight, nine, ten.

Osito, osito ¿puedes saltar?
Si, si ayúdame, ayúdame a contar.
Uno, dos, tres, cuatro, cinco,
seis, siete, ocho, nueve, diez.

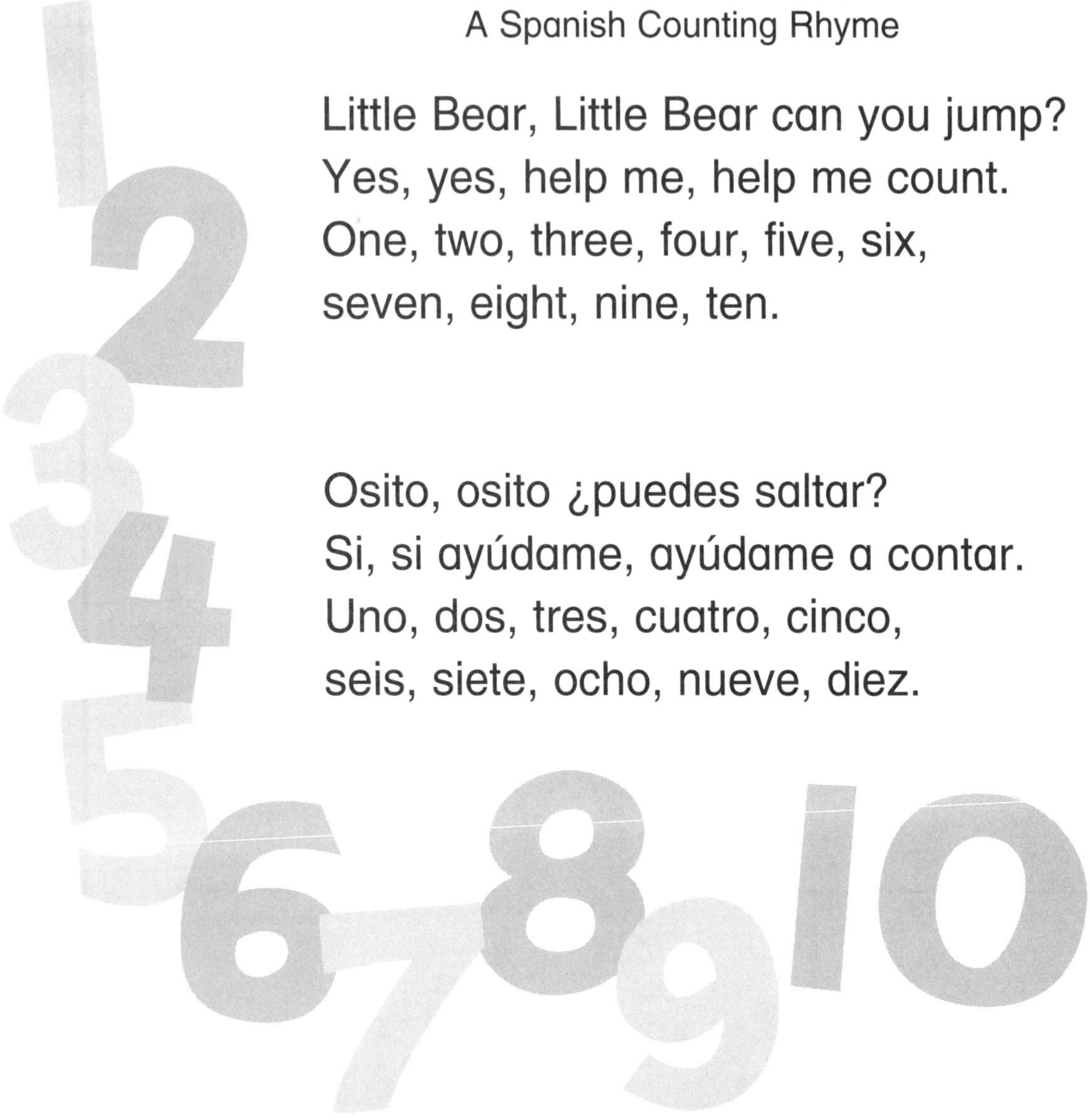

Hats

Baby Bear page 67

Read to Me . . .

Today we read and acted out *Little Bear, Little Bear*. Attached you will find a copy of the rhyme that we read. Ask me to tell you about it. Then let's read it together while I act it out. Ask me questions about the rhyme, like, *How old is Little Bear? Where do you think the rhyme takes place?*

Thank you for caring to read to me.

Itsy Bitsy Spider

The Itsy Bitsy Spider
Crawled up the waterspout.
Down came the rain
And washed the spider out.
Out came the sun
And dried up all the rain.
So the Itsy Bitsy Spider
Crawled up the spout again.

Hats

Spider page 69

Read to Me . . .

Today we read and acted out *Itsy Bitsy Spider*. Attached you will find a copy of the song that we sang and read. Ask me to tell you about it. Then let's read it together while I act it out. Ask me questions about the song, like, *Where do you think the spider was going?*

Thank you for caring to read to me.

____

Little Miss Muffet

Little Miss Muffet
Sat on a tuffet,
Eating her curds and whey.
Along came a spider,
Who sat down beside her.
And frightened Miss Muffet away!

Hats

Spider	page 69
Little Miss Muffet	page 70

Props

Spoon and Bowl "filled" with curds and whey	page 68

Read to Me . . .

Today we read and acted out *Little Miss Muffet.* Attached you will find a copy of the rhyme that we read and the props that we used. Ask me to tell you about it. Then let's read it together while I act it out. Ask me questions about the rhyme, like, *Did you know that a tuffet was like a stool? Are you afraid of spiders?*

Thank you for caring to read to me.

Anansi and Turtle

An Ashanti Tale

One day, Anansi the spider decided to cook himself a feast. He picked some of the biggest yams from his garden and baked them. They smelled delicious.

Anansi was just ready to sit down to eat when there was a knock at his door.

As he opened the door, he saw Turtle standing there.

"Oh, those yams smell so delicious," Turtle said. "Won't you share them with me?"

Anansi was not very happy. He really didn't want to share the yams but he didn't know what else to do. Then he thought of something.

"Come in, Turtle," Anansi said. "Sit down and help yourself."

Turtle sat down eagerly. He reached for one of the yams. But as he did so, Anansi said, "Wait. Your hands are dirty. You can't eat unless you wash your hands."

Turtle looked down at his hands. Anansi was right.

His hands were dirty. So Turtle got up and went to the river to wash his hands. All the way there and all the way back he just kept thinking of the delicious yams waiting for him at Anansi's house.

When Turtle got back, Anansi said, "I didn't want the yams to get cold so I started eating without you."

Turtle looked at the bowl of yams. The biggest ones were already gone but the ones that were left still looked and smelled delicious.

Once again, Turtle reached for one of the yams. And once again, Anansi said, "Wait. Your hands are still dirty. Didn't you wash them?"

Turtle looked at his hands. Anansi was right. They had been clean but they were dirty again. So Turtle went down to the river again. He washed his hands very carefully and then tried very hard on his way back to Anansi's house not to get them dirty again.

When Turtle got back, he sat down at the table and reached for the bowl of yams. But they were all gone.

Turtle realized that Anansi had tricked him.

But Turtle just smiled and said to Anansi, "Thank you for sharing your food with me. If you ever find yourself near my house, I hope you'll stop in and let me share my meal with you." And Turtle left.

As the days passed, Anansi thought more and more about Turtle's invitation. So one day he decided to take a walk to Turtle's house. Anansi put on his best jacket and started off for the river.

When he got there, he jumped into the river. But, instead of making it down to Turtle's underwater house, Anansi popped right back up to the surface. He was too light.

He tried again, but the same thing happened. Then Anansi had an idea.

He picked up a stone and put it in the pocket of his jacket. Then he picked up another stone and did the same thing. He picked up another and another until his pockets were filled with stones.

Anansi jumped into the water again. This time he sank right down to the bottom.

Turtle welcomed him to his home and they sat down at the table. There were so many delicious foods in front of him; Anansi didn't know where to start. But just as he reached out to take some, Turtle said to him, "In my house, we do not wear our jackets to the table."

Anansi started to remove his jacket. But as soon as he had taken it off, he popped right back up to the surface. He sat on the bank of the river and thought about all the wonderful foods he was missing.

A little while later, Turtle came up to sit down next to him. “I really enjoyed that meal,” Turtle said. “It wouldn't have been the same without you. We'll have to do it again some day.” And then he smiled.

Hats

Spider page 69

Turtle page 61

Props

Spoon and Bowl “filled” with yams page 68

Read to Me . . .

Today we read and acted out *Anansi and Turtle.* Attached you will find a copy of the story that we read and the props that we used. Ask me to tell you about it. Then let's read it together while I act it out. Ask me questions about the story, like, *Who is my favorite character? Where do you think the story took place?*

Thank you for caring to read to me.

There Was a Little Turtle

There was a little turtle,
He lived in a box.
He swam in a puddle,
He climbed on the rocks.

He snapped at a mosquito,
He snapped at a flea,
He snapped at a minnow,
And he snapped at me!

He caught the mosquito,
He caught the flea,
He caught the minnow,
But he didn't catch me!

Hats

Turtle	page 61
Mosquito	page 71
Flea	page 72
Minnow	page 73

Read to Me . . .

Today we read and acted out *There Was a Little Turtle*. Attached you will find a copy of the poem that we read. Ask me to tell you about it. Then let's read it together while I act it out. Ask me questions about the poem, like, *Who did the turtle snap at first?*

Thank you for caring to read to me.

____

Little Fish

A Spanish Nursery Rhyme

Little fish move in the water.
They swim, swim, swim.
They fly, fly, fly.
Little ones, little ones,
Fly, fly, fly.
Swim, swim, swim.

Los pececitos nadan en el agua,
nadan, nadan, nadan.
Vuelan, vuelan, vuelan.
Son chiquititos, chiquititos.
Vuelan, vuelan, vuelan.
Nadan, nadan, nadan.

Hats

Minnow page 73

Read to Me . . .

Today we read and acted out *Little Fish*. Attached you will find a copy of the rhyme that we read and the props that we used. Ask me to tell you about it. Then let's read it together while I act it out. Ask me questions about the rhyme, like, *what did the fish do first?*

Thank you for caring to read to me.

____

Three Little Kittens

Three little kittens,
They lost their mittens,
And they began to cry,
"Oh, Mother Dear, we sadly fear
Our mittens we have lost."
"Lost your mittens!
You naughty kittens!
Then you shall have no pie."
"Meow, meow, meow, meow!"
"Then you shall have no pie."

Three little kittens,
They found their mittens,
And they began to cry,
"Oh, Mother Dear, see here, see here
Our mittens we have found."
"Found your mittens!
You lovely kittens!
Then you shall have some pie."
"Meow, meow, meow, meow!"
"Then you shall have some pie."

Three little kittens,
Put on their mittens,
And soon ate up the pie.
"Oh, Mother Dear, we greatly fear,
Our mittens we have soiled."
"Soiled your mittens!
You naughty kittens!"
Then they began to sigh.
"Meow, meow, meow, meow!"
Then they began to sigh.

Three little kittens,
They washed their mittens,
And hung them out to dry.
"Oh, Mother Dear, see here, see here
Our mittens we have washed."
"Washed your mittens!
You lovely kittens!
But I smell a mouse close by."
"Meow, meow, meow, meow!"
"But I smell a mouse close by."

Hats

Mother Cat	page 74
Kitten	page 75
Mouse	page 91

Props

Mittens	page 76

Read to Me . . .

Today we read and acted out *Three Little Kittens*. Attached you will find a copy of the rhyme that we read and the props that we used. Ask me to tell you about it. Then let's read it together while I act it out. Ask me questions about the rhyme, like, *How many kittens were there? Have you ever done naughty things like those kittens?*

Thank you for caring to read to me.

____

Hey Diddle Diddle

Hey diddle diddle,
The cat and the fiddle,
The cow jumped over the moon.

The little dog laughed
To see such sport,
And the dish ran away with the spoon.

Hats

Cat	page 74
Fiddle	page 77
Cow	page 78
Dog	page 80
Dish	page 81
Spoon	page 82

Props

Moon	page 79

Read to Me . . .

Today we read and acted out *Hey Diddle Diddle*. Attached you will find a copy of the rhyme that we read and the props that we used. Ask me to tell you about it. Then let's read it together while I act it out. Ask me questions about the rhyme, like, *Who is your favorite character?*

Thank you for caring to read to me.

____

The Ugly Duckling

Once upon a time, there was a mother duck who lived near a lake. One by one the eggs she was sitting on began to hatch. Out of each egg popped a fluffy yellow duckling.

Soon there was just one egg left. Finally it hatched. But instead of fluffy yellow feathers, this duckling had gray ones.

"What an ugly little duckling you are!" the mother duck said. His brothers and sisters began to tease the ugly little duckling. They didn't want to play with him. As the days went by, the poor little duckling became more and more unhappy.

So one day, the ugly little duckling decided to run away. He went farther than he had ever been before with his mother or any of his brothers and sisters. He came to a pond and started searching through the reeds for food.

He saw some wild ducks flying by. They stopped to ask, "What kind of bird are you?"

"I'm a duck," said the ugly little duckling.
"What a funny looking duck you are!" the ducks said as they flew away.

"If nobody wants me, then I'll hide here forever," said the ugly little duckling.

Then one day he looked up and saw some beautiful birds flying south. They had long slender necks, yellow beaks, and large wings.

"If only I could look like them, just for a day!" said the ugly duckling. But the big white swans were far away by this time.

The ugly little duckling was very lonely but he stayed where he was all winter long. It was very, very cold.

One day it started to feel warmer. Springtime was finally coming. The ugly duckling stretched out his wings. Over the winter he had grown bigger and stronger.

He saw the swans flying back north. They landed on the pond.

"Come and join us," they said to the ugly duckling.

"You want me to join you?" the ugly duckling asked. "But I'm just an ugly duckling."

"You're not a duckling. You're a swan, just like us," said one of the swans.

The duckling looked at himself in the water. They were right. He wasn't an ugly duckling, but a beautiful white swan just like the others.

He held his long slender neck up high. He swam around the pond proudly with the other swans. And he lived happily ever after.

Hats

Mother Duck	page 83
Ugly Duckling	page 84
Duckling	page 85
Ugly Duckling Changing	page 86
Swan	page 87

Read to Me . . .

Today we read and acted out *The Ugly Duckling*. Attached you will find a copy of the story that we read. Ask me to tell you about it. Then let's read it together while I act it out. Ask me questions about the story, like, *How would you feel if you were the duckling?*

Thank you for caring to read to me.

____

The Crab and Its Mother

An Aesop's Fable

One morning, a mother crab was walking with her daughter, at the bottom of the sea.

"Why do you walk sideways like that?" the mother crab asked her child. "You should walk in a straight line."

"But Mother," the little crab said, "This is the way you walk. And I learned to walk from you. Can you please show me how you want me to walk? Then I'll walk that way, too."

So the mother crab said to the little crab, "Watch carefully."

Then she tried to step forward instead of sideways. But as hard as she tried, she couldn't do it. "Oh well," she finally said to the little crab. "I guess I can't tell you how to walk if I can't do it myself."

And with that the two continued on their sideways walk at the bottom of the sea.

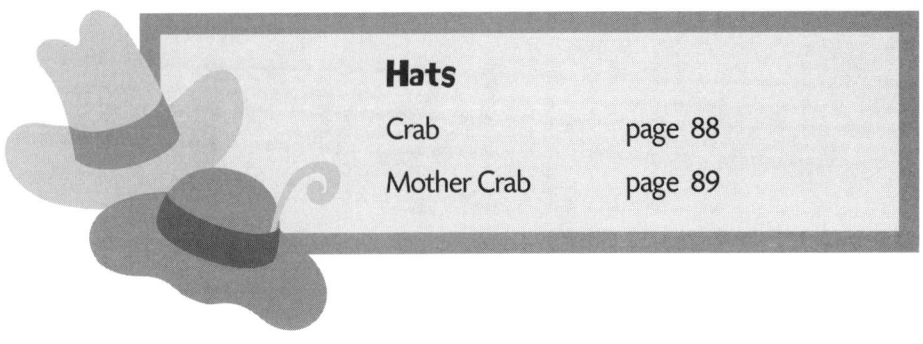

Hats

Crab page 88

Mother Crab page 89

Read to Me . . .

Today we read and acted out *The Crab and Its Mother*. Attached you will find a copy of the story that we read. Ask me to tell you about it. Then let's read it together while I act it out. Ask me questions about the story, like, *What is something you learned to do by watching a grownup? Where do you think you would find crabs?*

Thank you for caring to read to me.

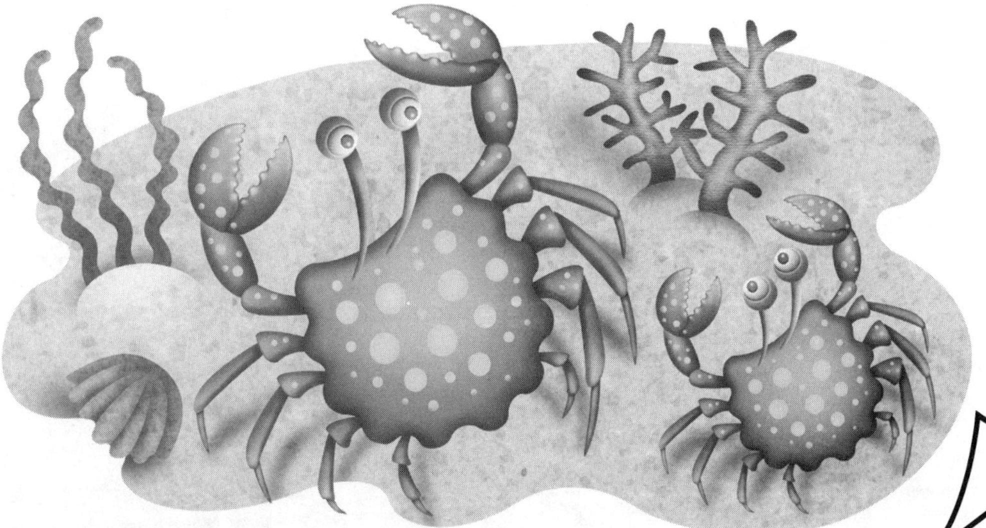

The Lion and the Mouse

An Aesop's Fable

One day, a lion lay asleep in the jungle. A small mouse climbed up on the lion's tail ran across the lion's back, and ran across its face. The lion awoke and down came its huge paw over the little mouse.

"Please," said the mouse. "Let me go. If you do, I'll come back and help you someday."

The lion began to laugh. "How could you ever do anything to help me? You are so tiny," the lion said. And he laughed and laughed.

But the lion decided the mouse wasn't much of a meal anyway. So he took his paw off the mouse and the mouse quickly ran away.

Shortly after that, the lion was caught by hunters. They tied him up with rope and went to find a wagon in which to carry him. The unhappy lion roared and roared.

The little mouse heard him roaring and came to help. With his sharp teeth, the little mouse gnawed at the rope until the rope broke.

The lion was free once again.

“Was I not right?” asked the little mouse.

“You were,” said the lion. “You did help me even though I am so big and you are so little. Thank you.”

Hats
Lion page 90
Mouse page 91

Read to Me . . .

Today we read and acted out *The Lion and the Mouse*. Attached you will find a copy of the story that we read. Ask me to tell you about it. Then let's read it together while I act it out. Ask me questions about the story, like, *Why do you think the lion roared and roared? What have you done to help someone bigger and stronger than you?*

Thank you for caring to read to me.

Old MacDonald

Old MacDonald had a farm, E I E I O!
And on his farm he had some chicks, E I E I O!
With a chick-chick here,
And a chick-chick there
Here a chick, there a chick,
Everywhere a chick-chick
Old MacDonald had a farm, E I E I O!

Old MacDonald had a farm, E I E I O!
And on his farm he had some cows, E I E I O!
With a moo-moo here,
And a moo-moo there
Here a moo, there a moo,
Everywhere a moo-moo
Old MacDonald had a farm, E I E I O!

Old MacDonald had a farm, E I E I O!
And on his farm he had some pigs, E I E I O!
With an oink-oink here,
And an oink-oink there
Here an oink, there an oink,
Everywhere an oink-oink
Old MacDonald had a farm, E I E I O!

Old MacDonald had a farm, E I E I O!
And on his farm he had some horses, E I E I O!
With a neigh-neigh here,
And a neigh-neigh there
Here a neigh, there a neigh,
Everywhere a neigh-neigh
Old MacDonald had a farm, E I E I O!

Old MacDonald had a farm, E I E I O!
And on his farm he had some ducks, E I E I O!
With a quack-quack here,
And a quack-quack there
Here a quack, there a quack,
Everywhere a quack-quack
Old MacDonald had a farm, E I E I O!

Old MacDonald had a farm, E I E I O!
And on his farm he had some sheep, E I E I O!
With a baa-baa here,
And a baa-baa there
Here a baa, there a baa,
Everywhere a baa-baa
Old MacDonald had a farm, E I E I O!

Hats

Chick	pages 92
Cow	pages 78
Pig	pages 93
Horse	pages 94
Dog	pages 80
Cat	pages 74
Duck	pages 85

Read to Me . . .

Today we read and acted out *Old MacDonald.* Attached you will find a copy of the song that we sang and read. Ask me to tell you about it. Then let's read it together while I act it out. Ask me questions about the song, like, *Who is my favorite character? Where do you think the story took place? What other animals might be on a farm?*

Thank you for caring to read to me.

____

There's a Cow on the Mountain

A Chinese Nursery Rhyme

There's a cow on the mountain,
so the old poem goes,
On her legs are four feet,
on her feet are eight toes.
Her head is in front
and her tail is in back.
She nibbles on grass
and on hay for a snack.

Hats

Cow	pages 78
Cow's tail	page 95

Read to Me . . .

Today we read and acted out *There's a Cow on the Mountain.* Attached you will find a copy of the rhyme that we read and the props that we used. Ask me to tell you about it. Then let's read it together while I act it out. Ask me questions about the rhyme, like, *Where was the cow?*

Thank you for caring to read to me.

____

Bear

Reproduce, color, cut, align and assemble

Turtle

Reproduce, color, cut, align and assemble

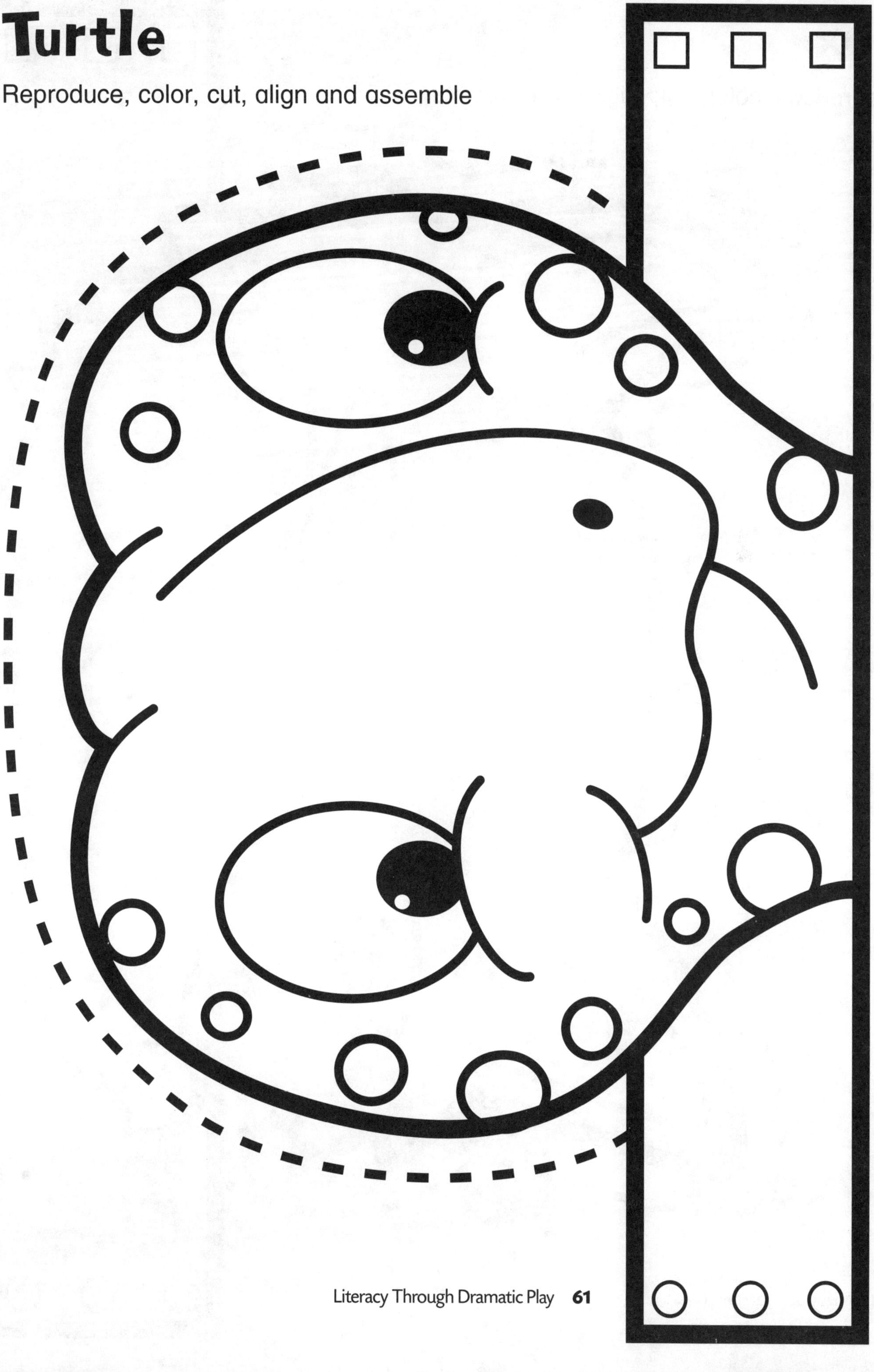

Fox

Reproduce, color, cut, align and assemble

Deer Reproduce, color, cut, align and assemble

Goldilocks

Reproduce, color, cut, align and assemble

Papa Bear

Reproduce, color, cut, align and assemble

Momma Bear

Reproduce, color, cut, align and assemble

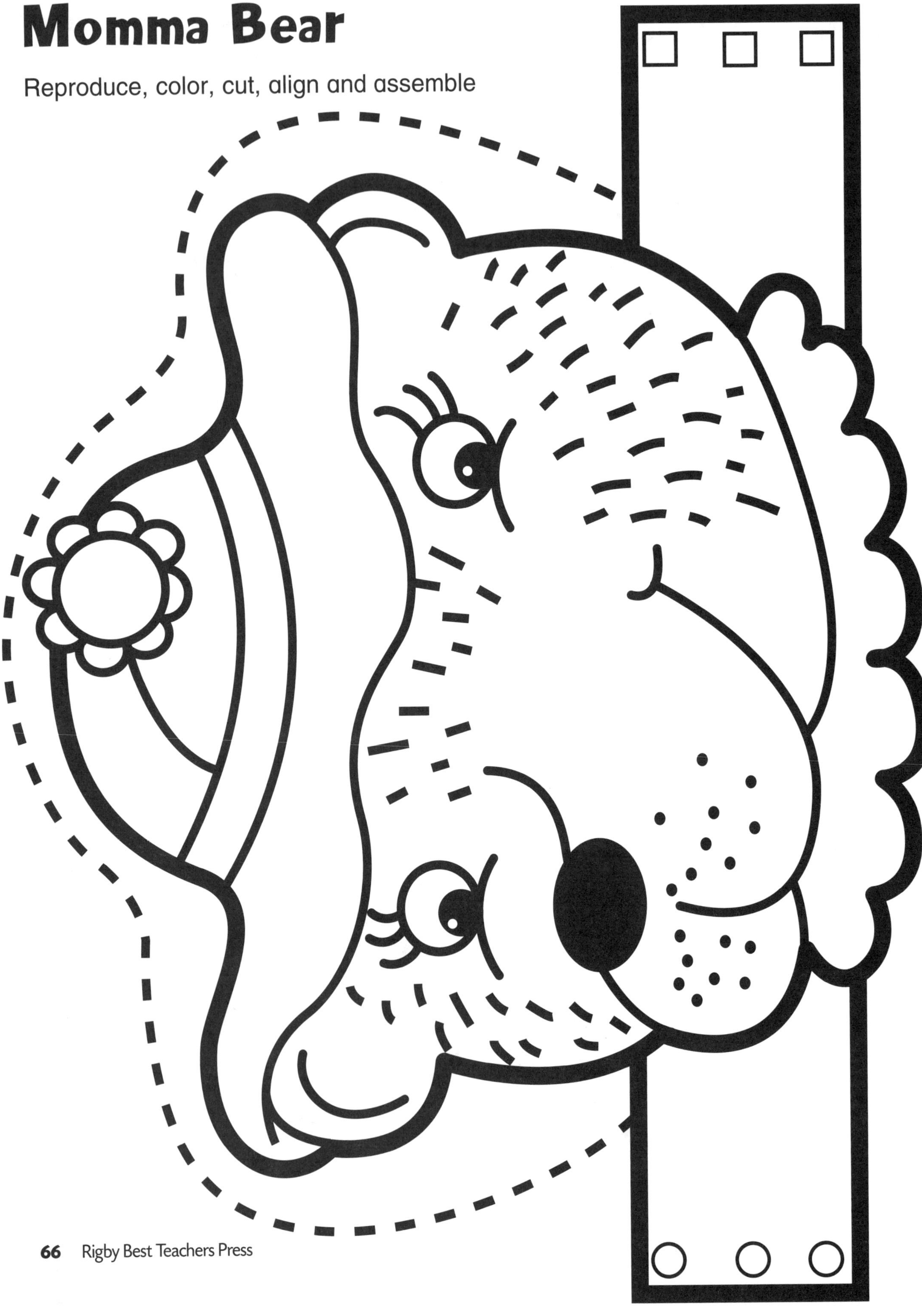

Baby Bear

Reproduce, color, cut, align and assemble

Spoon and Bowl

Reproduce, color, cut, align and assemble

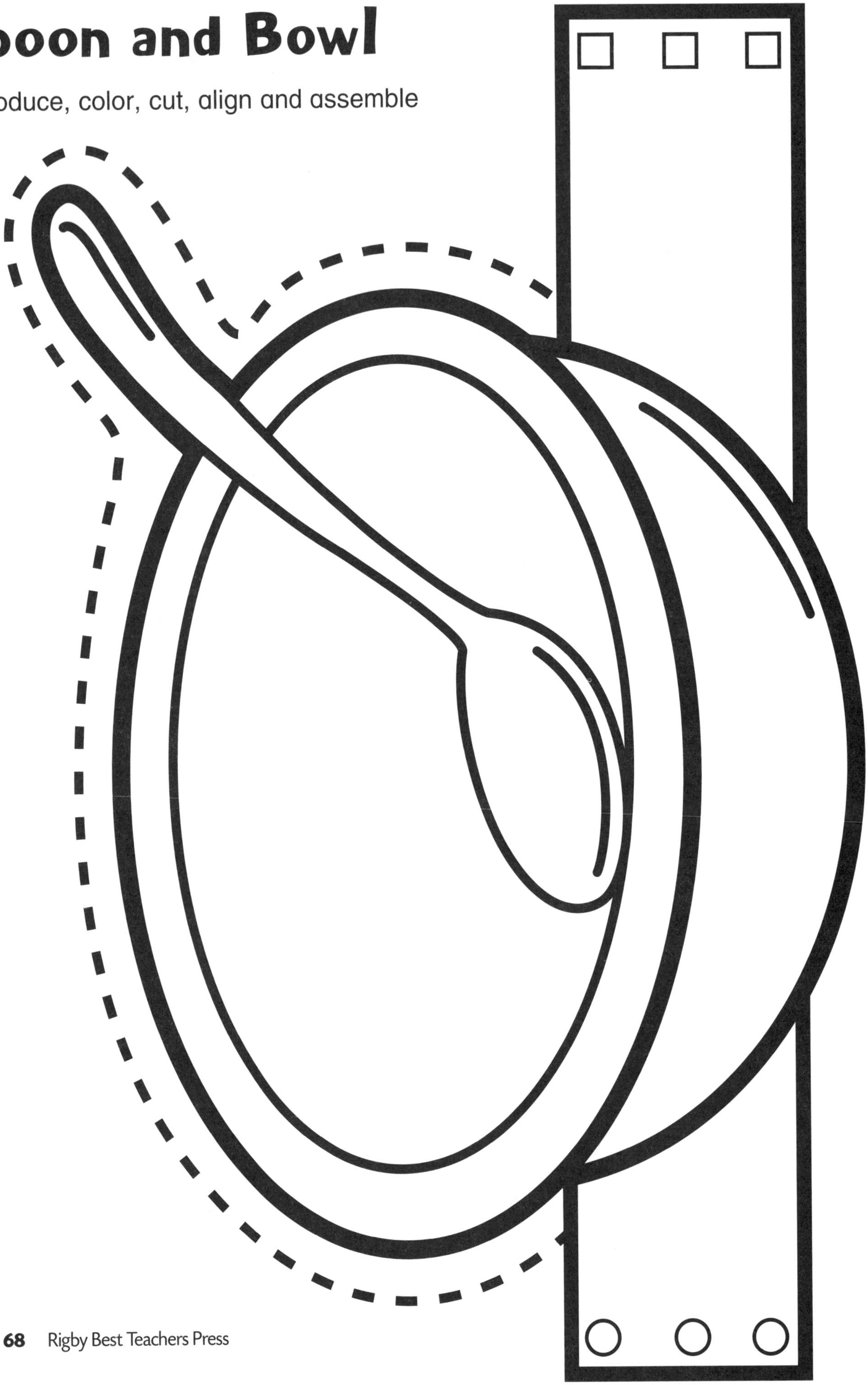

Spider

Reproduce, color, cut, align and assemble

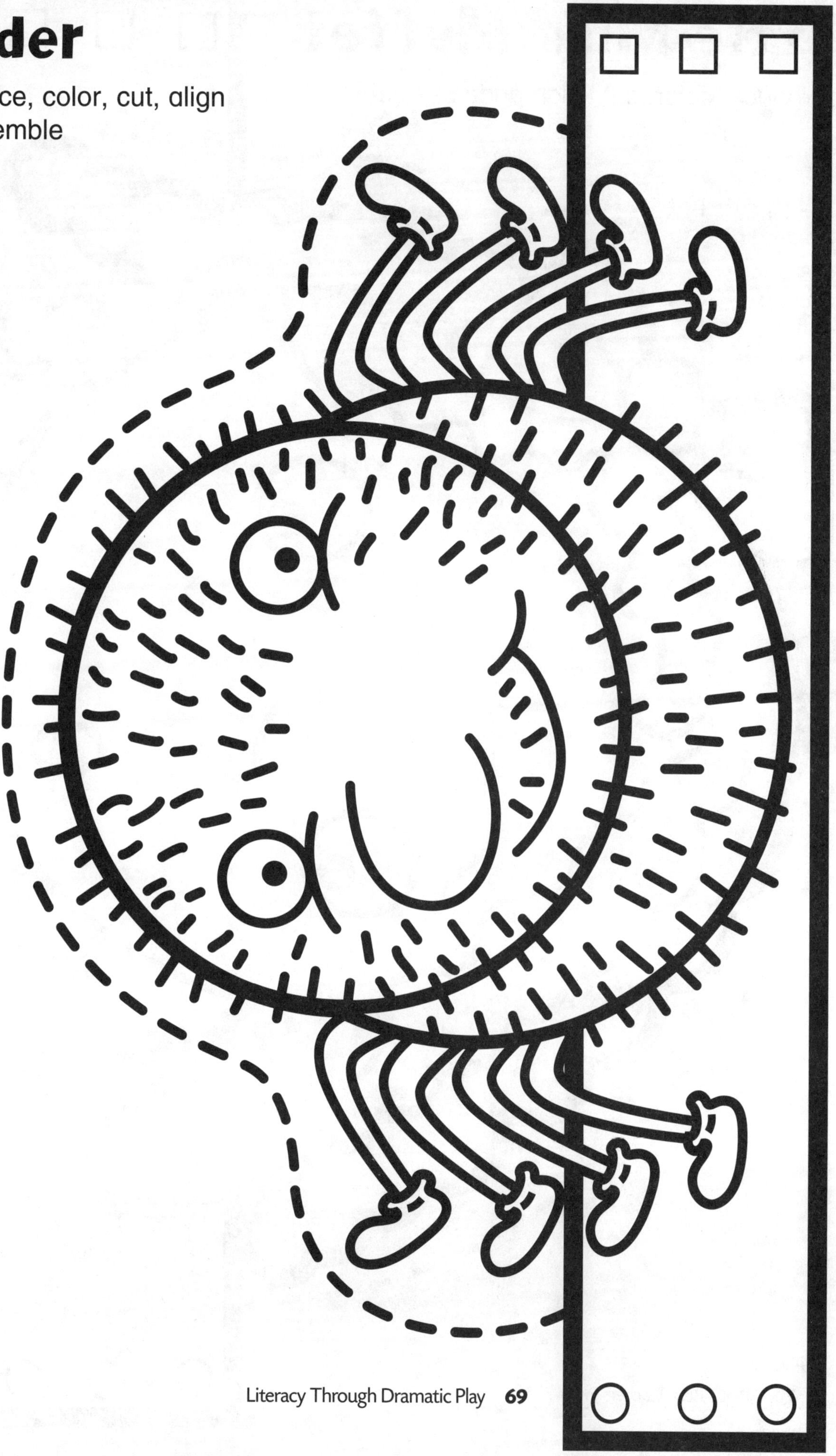

Little Miss Muffet

Reproduce, color, cut, align and assemble

Mosquito

Reproduce, color, cut, align and assemble

Flea

Reproduce, color, cut, align and assemble

Minnow

Reproduce, color, cut, align and assemble

Mother Cat

Reproduce, color, cut, align and assemble

Kitten

Reproduce, color, cut, align and assemble

Mittens

Reproduce, color, cut, align and assemble

Fiddle

Reproduce, color, cut, align and assemble

Cow

Reproduce, color, cut, align and assemble

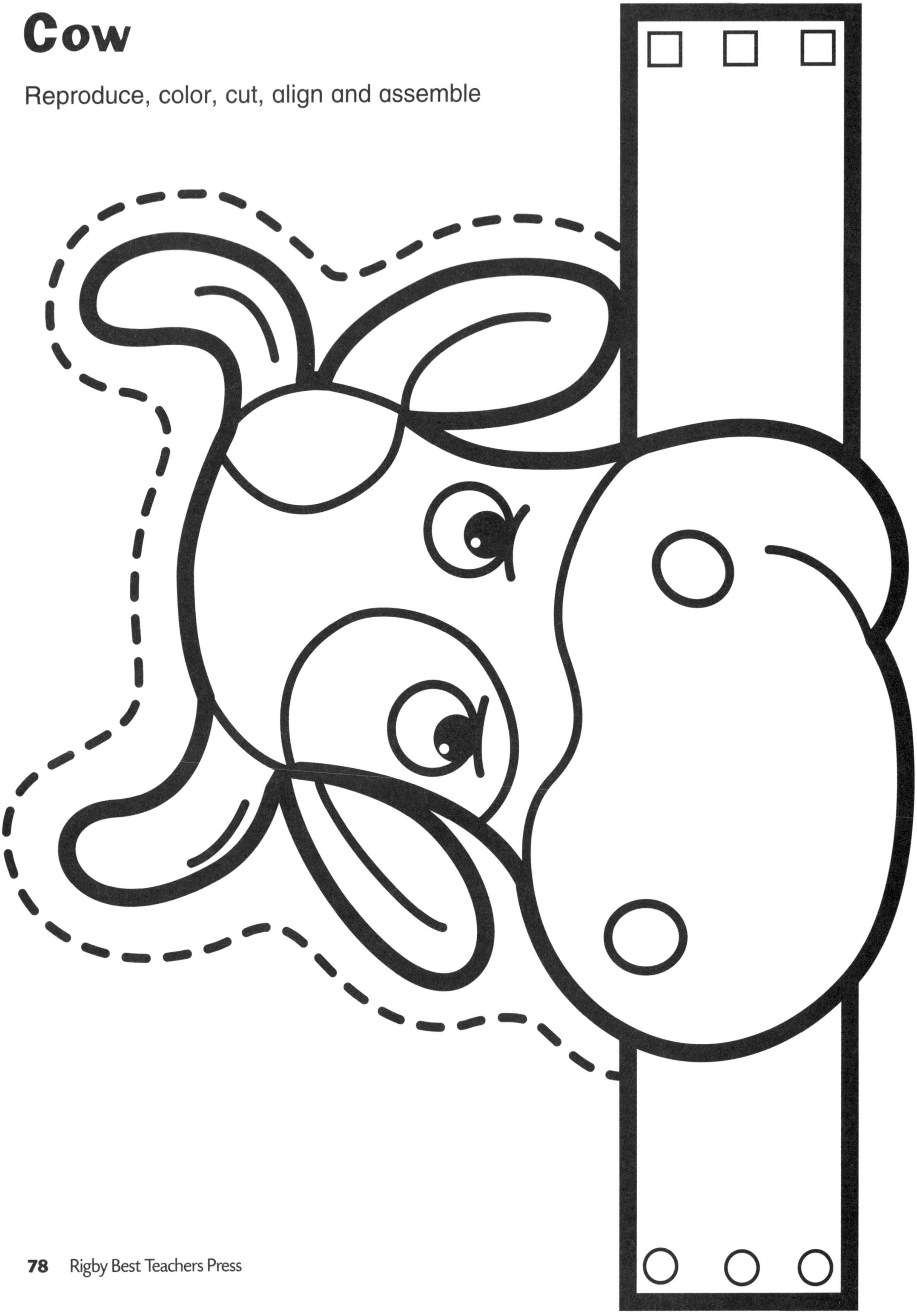

Moon

Reproduce, color, cut, align and assemble

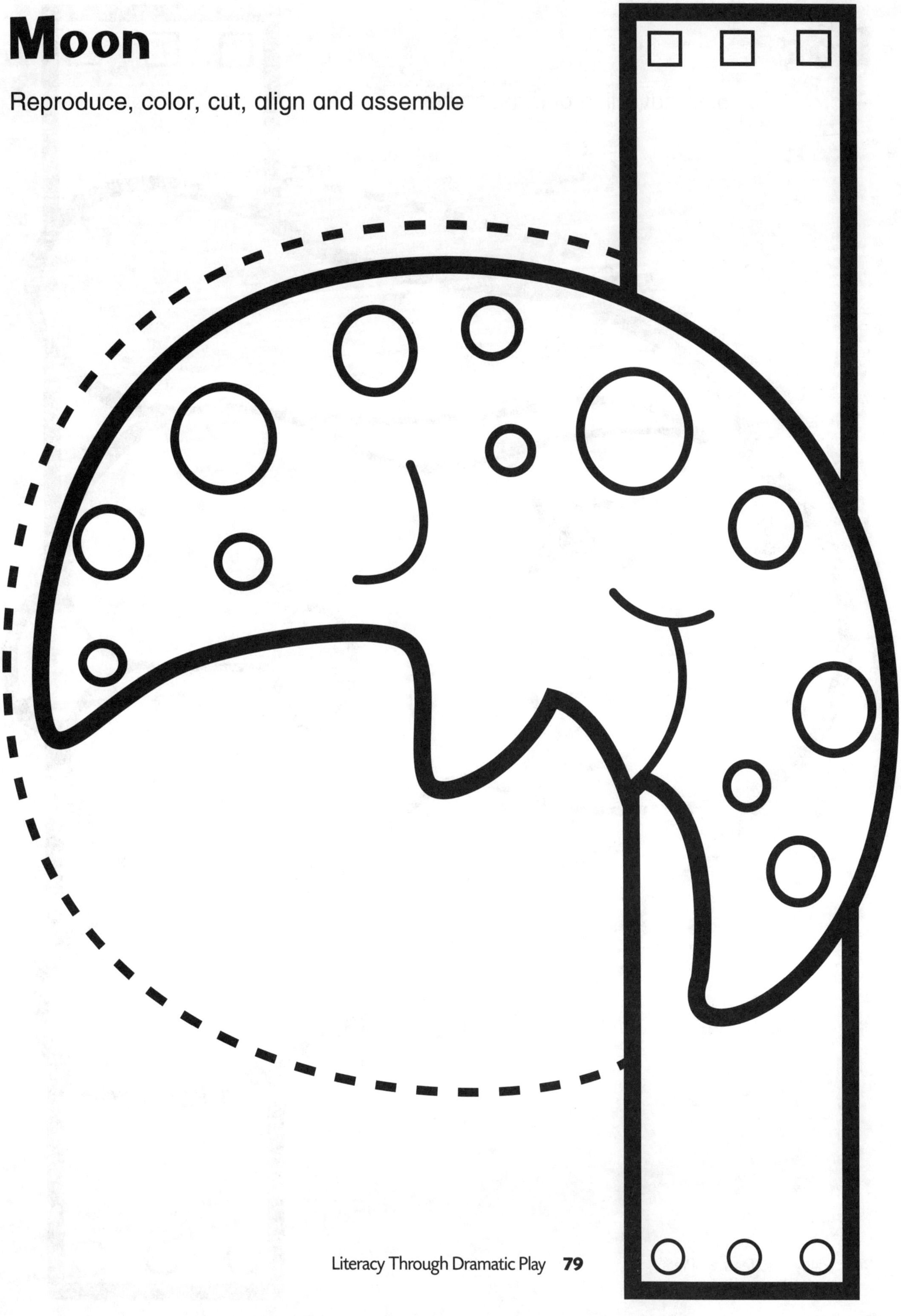

Dog

Reproduce, color, cut, align and assemble

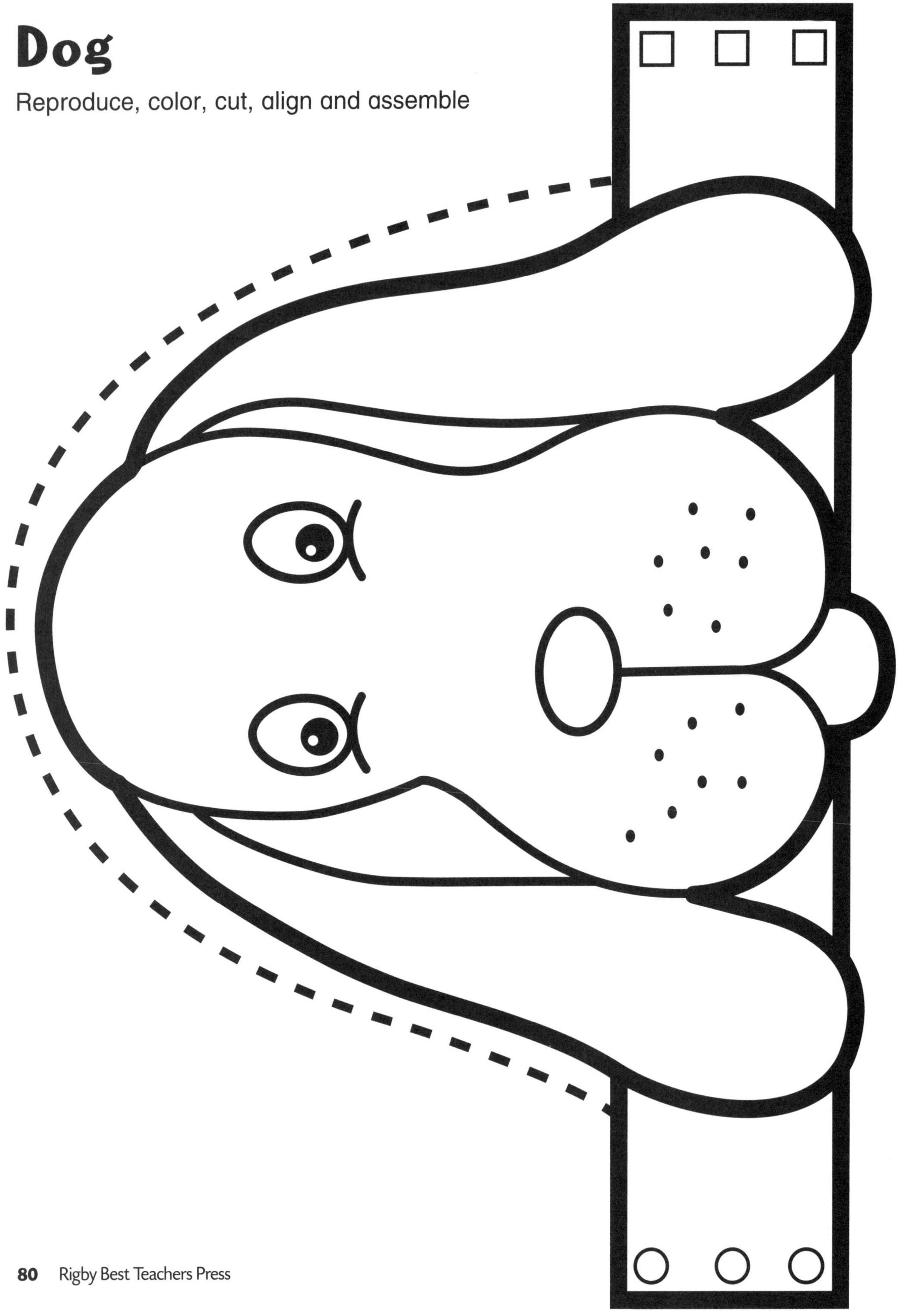

Dish

Reproduce, color, cut, align and assemble

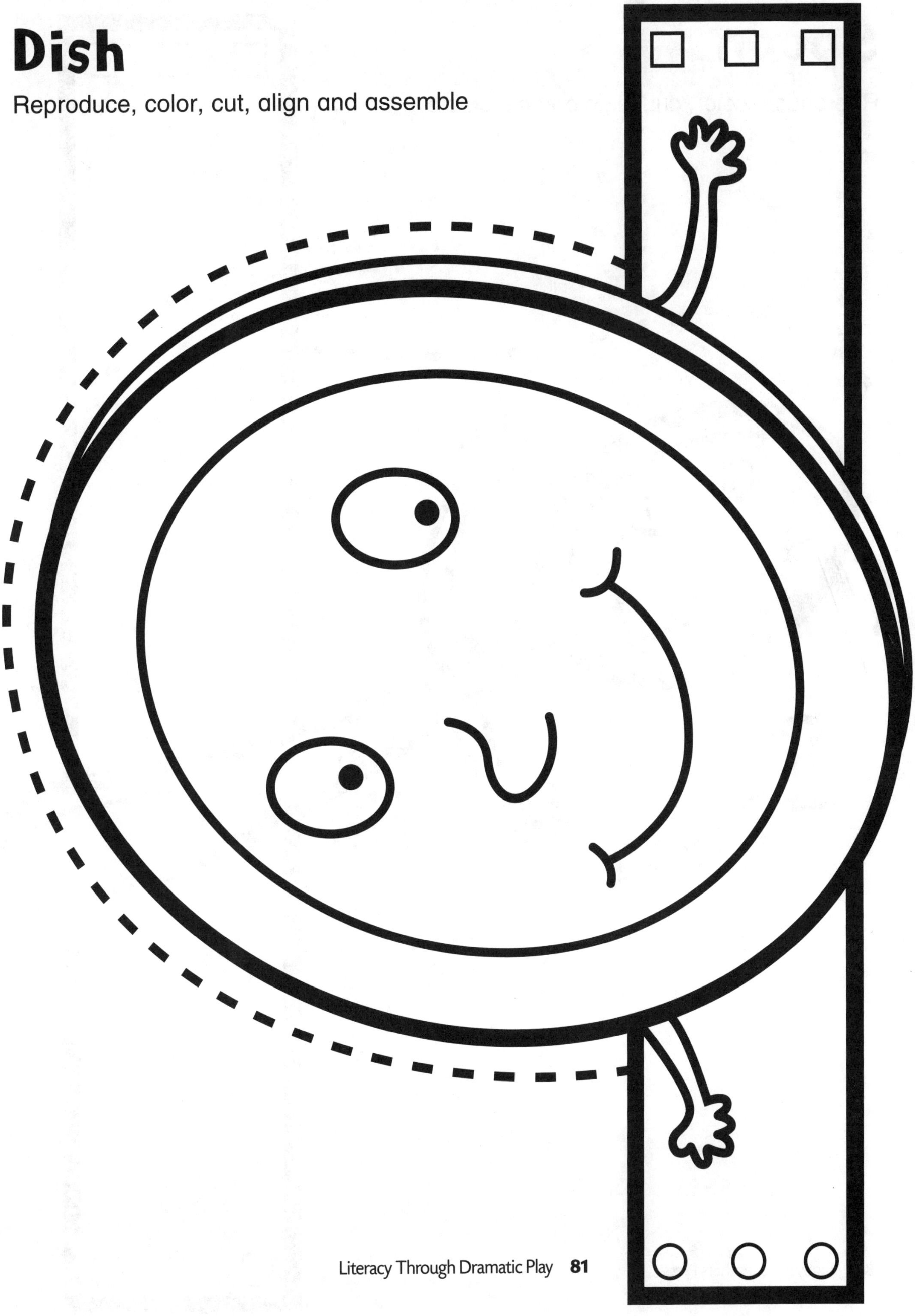

Spoon

Reproduce, color, cut, align and assemble

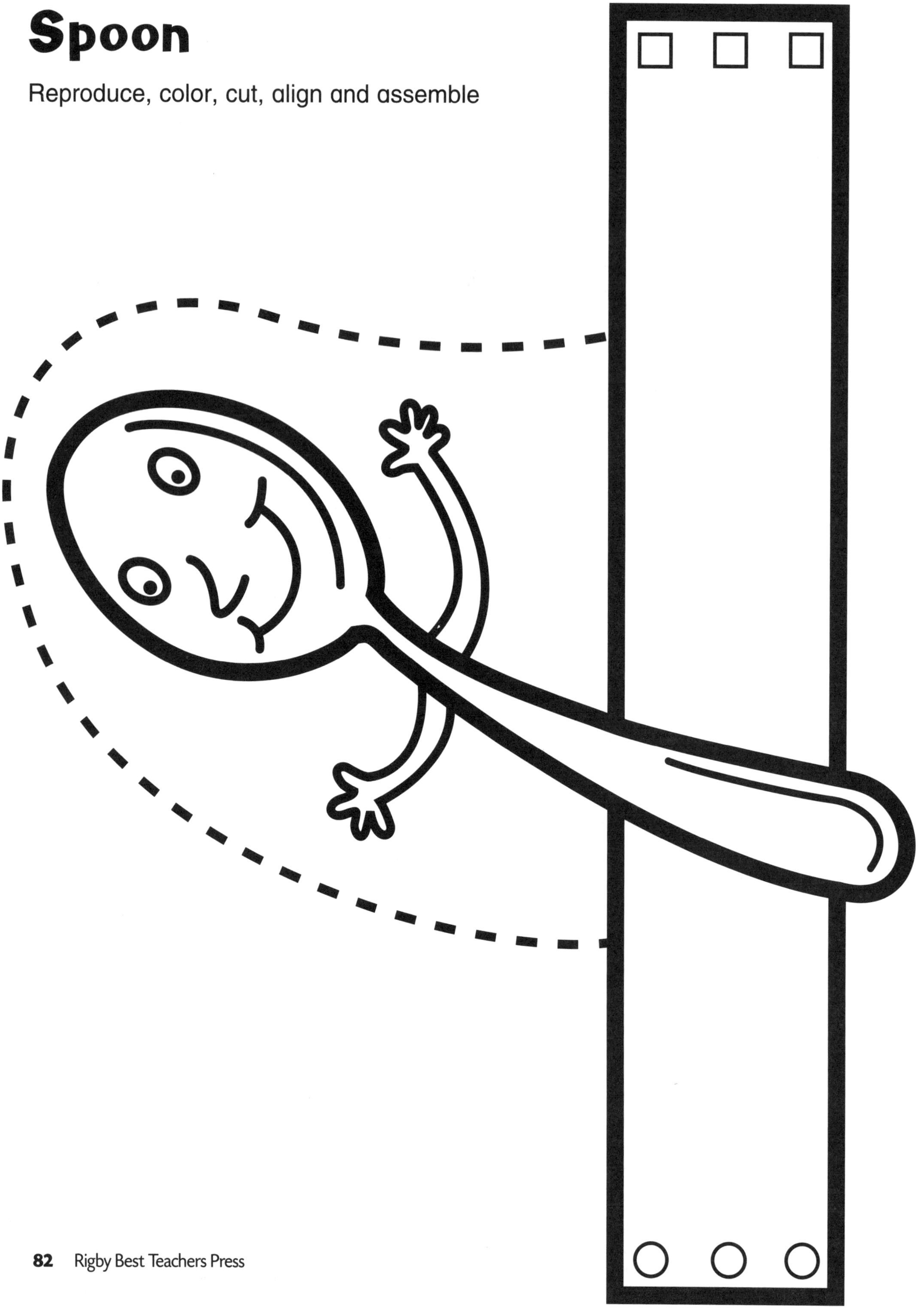

Mother Duck

Reproduce, color, cut, align and assemble

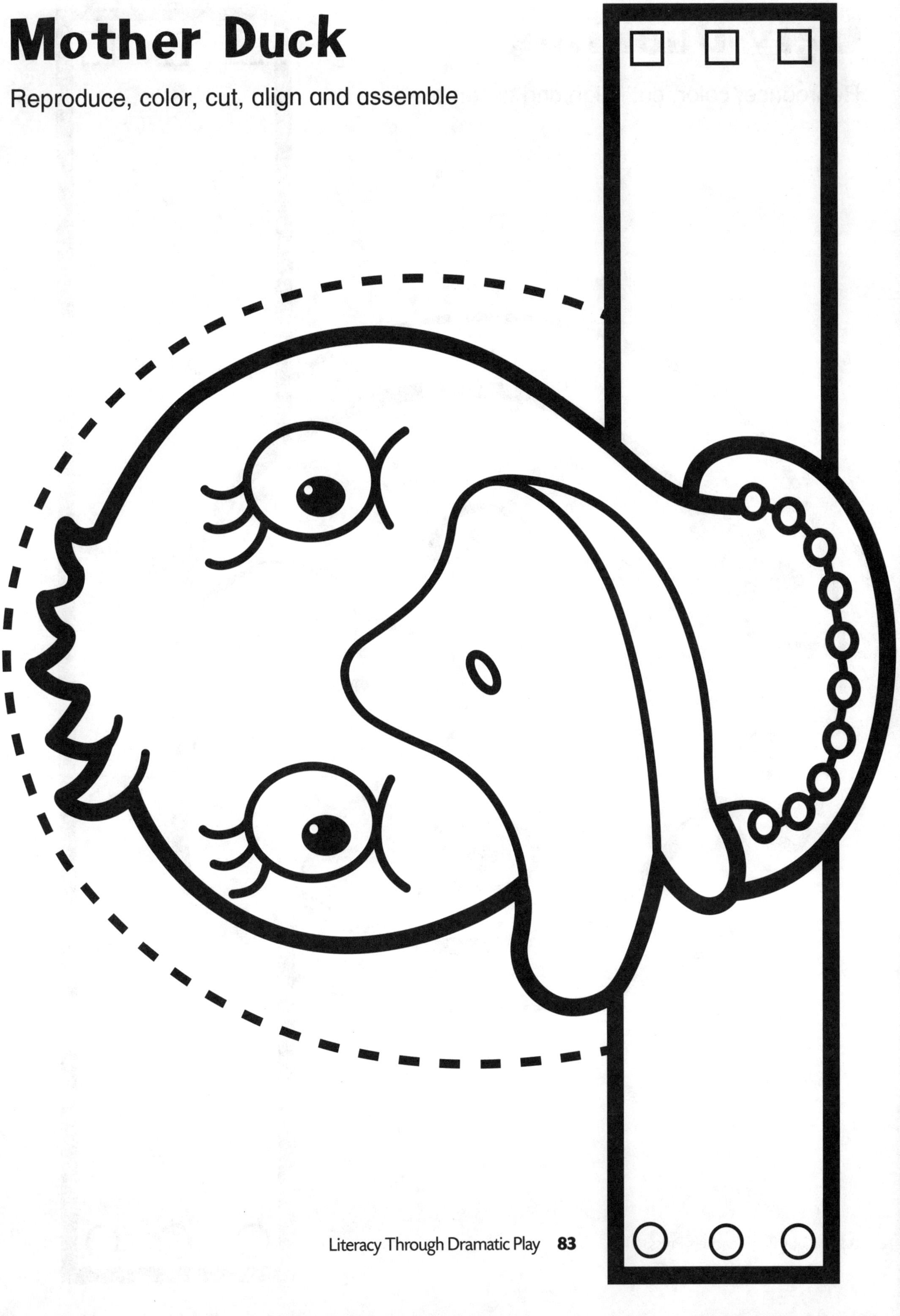

Ugly Duckling

Reproduce, color, cut, align and assemble

Duckling

Reproduce, color, cut, align and assemble

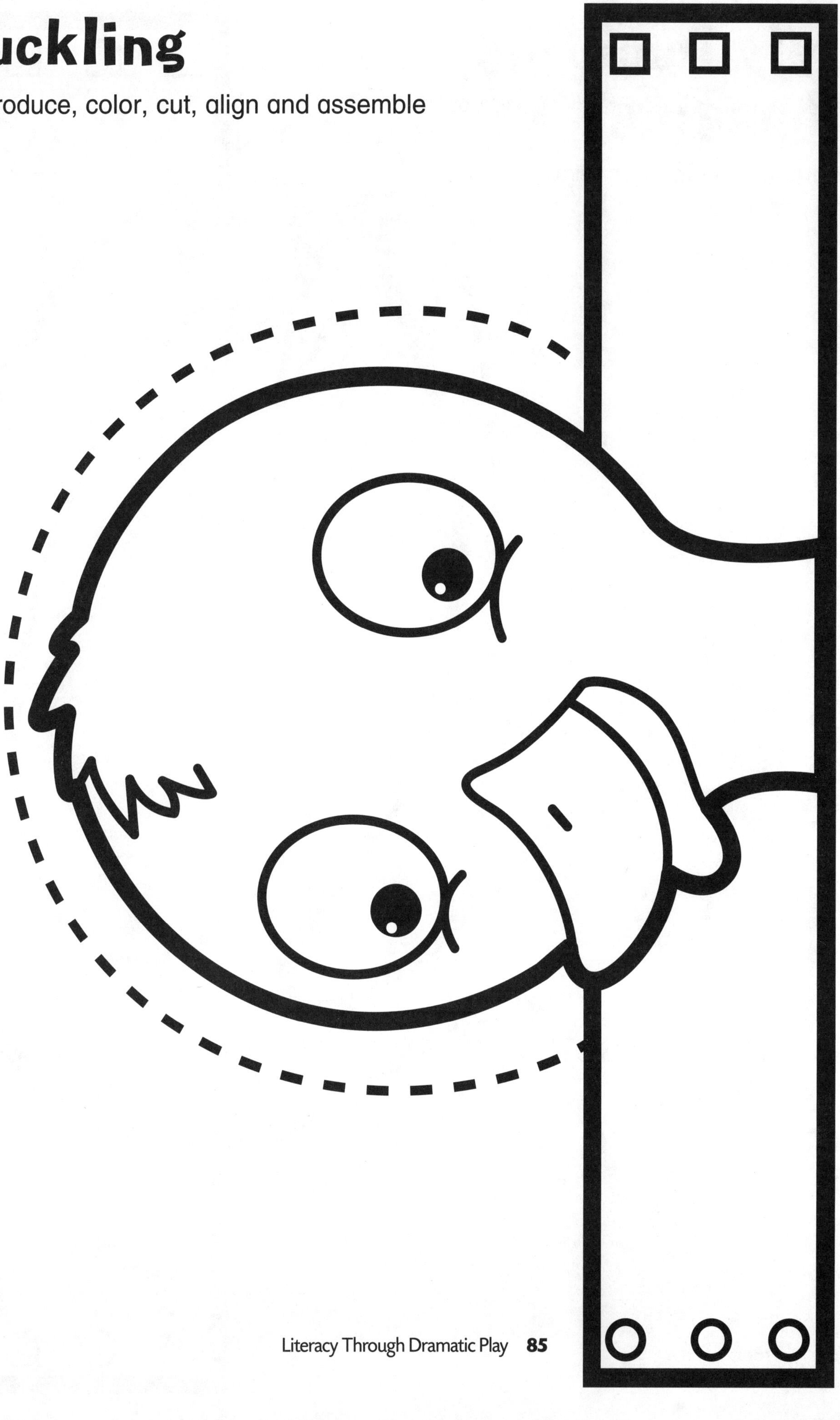

Ugly Duckling Changing

Reproduce, color, cut, align and assemble

Swan

Reproduce, color, cut, align and assemble

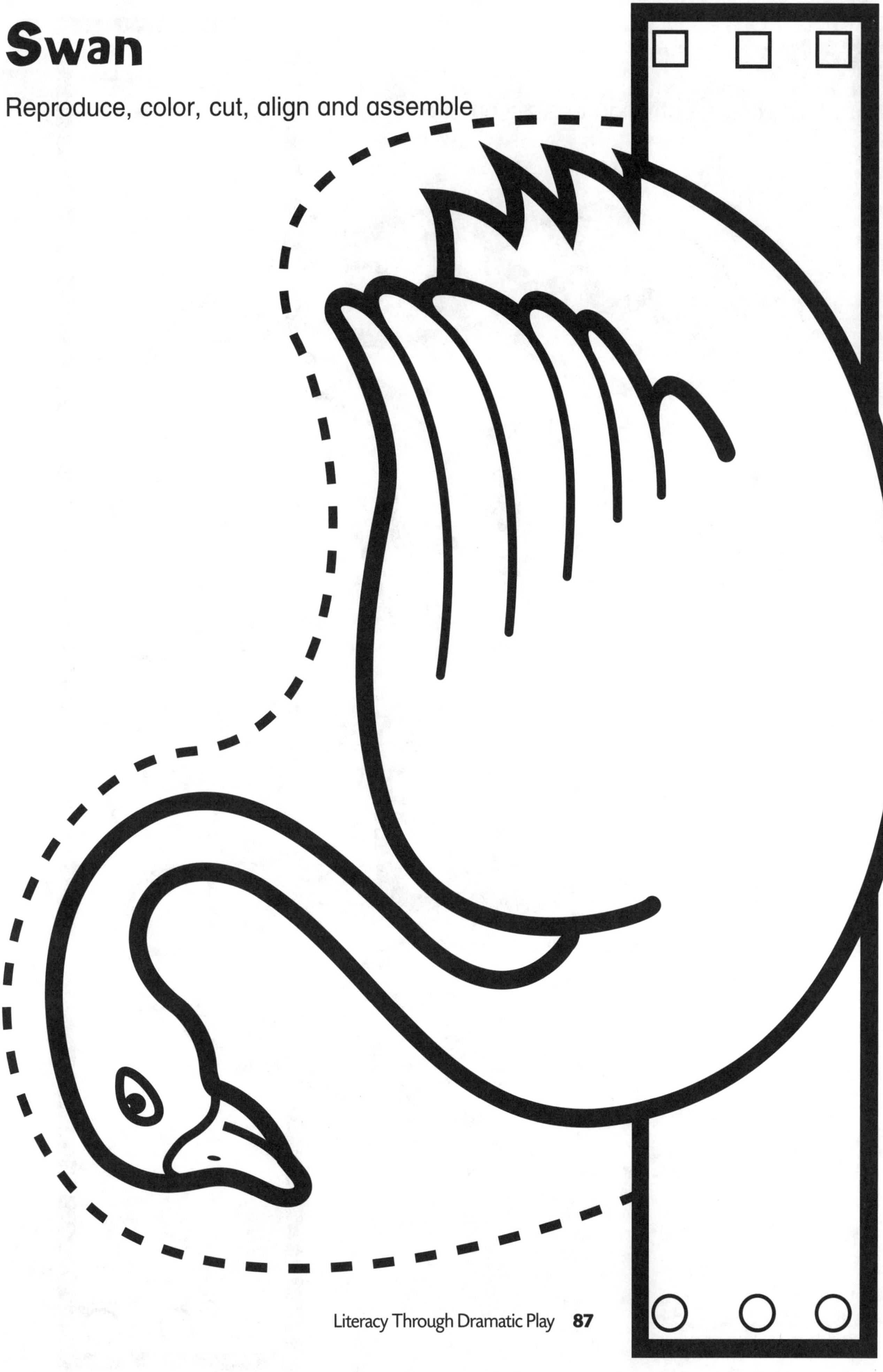

Crab

Reproduce, color, cut, align and assemble

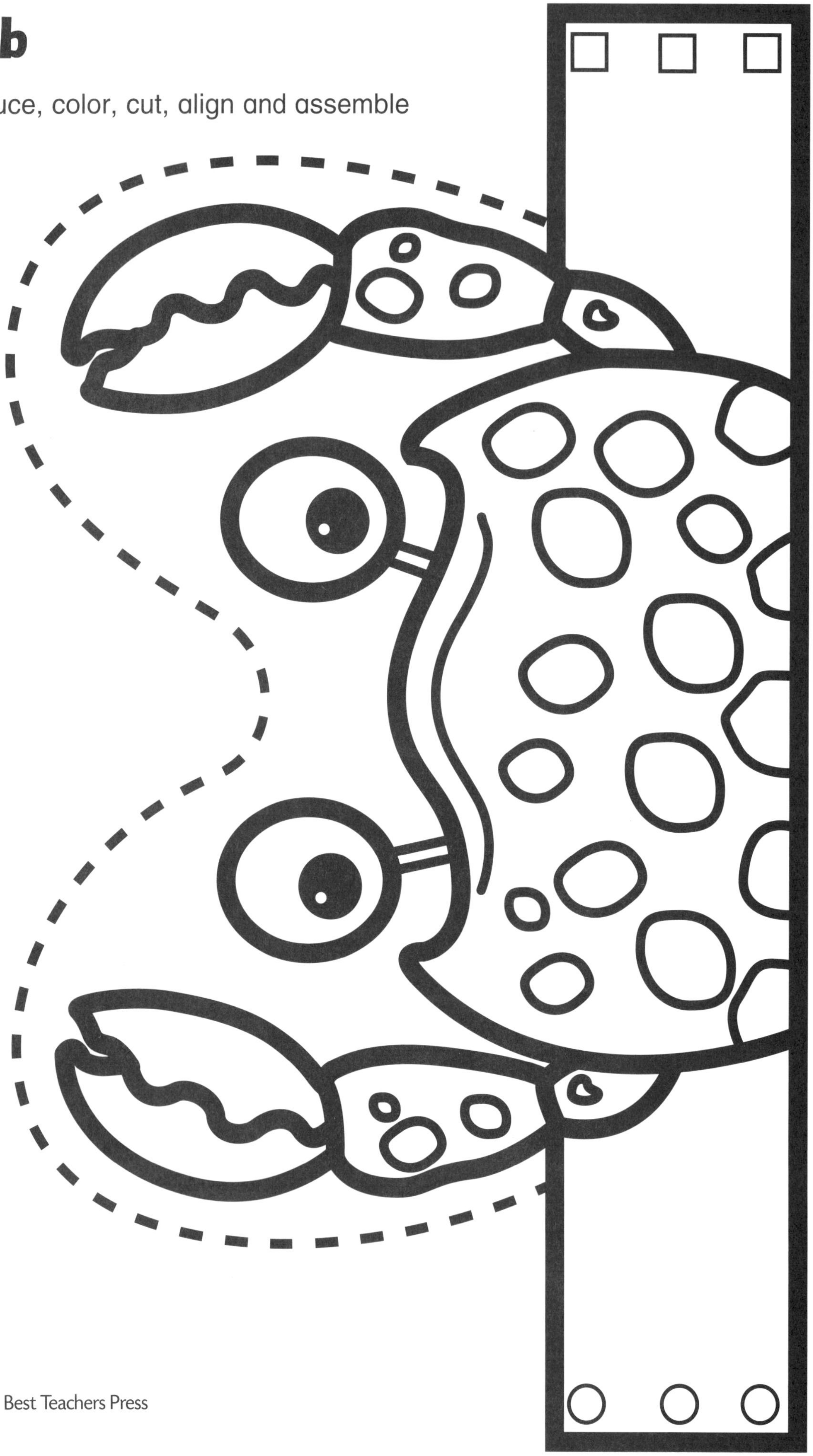

Mother Crab

Reproduce, color, cut, align and assemble

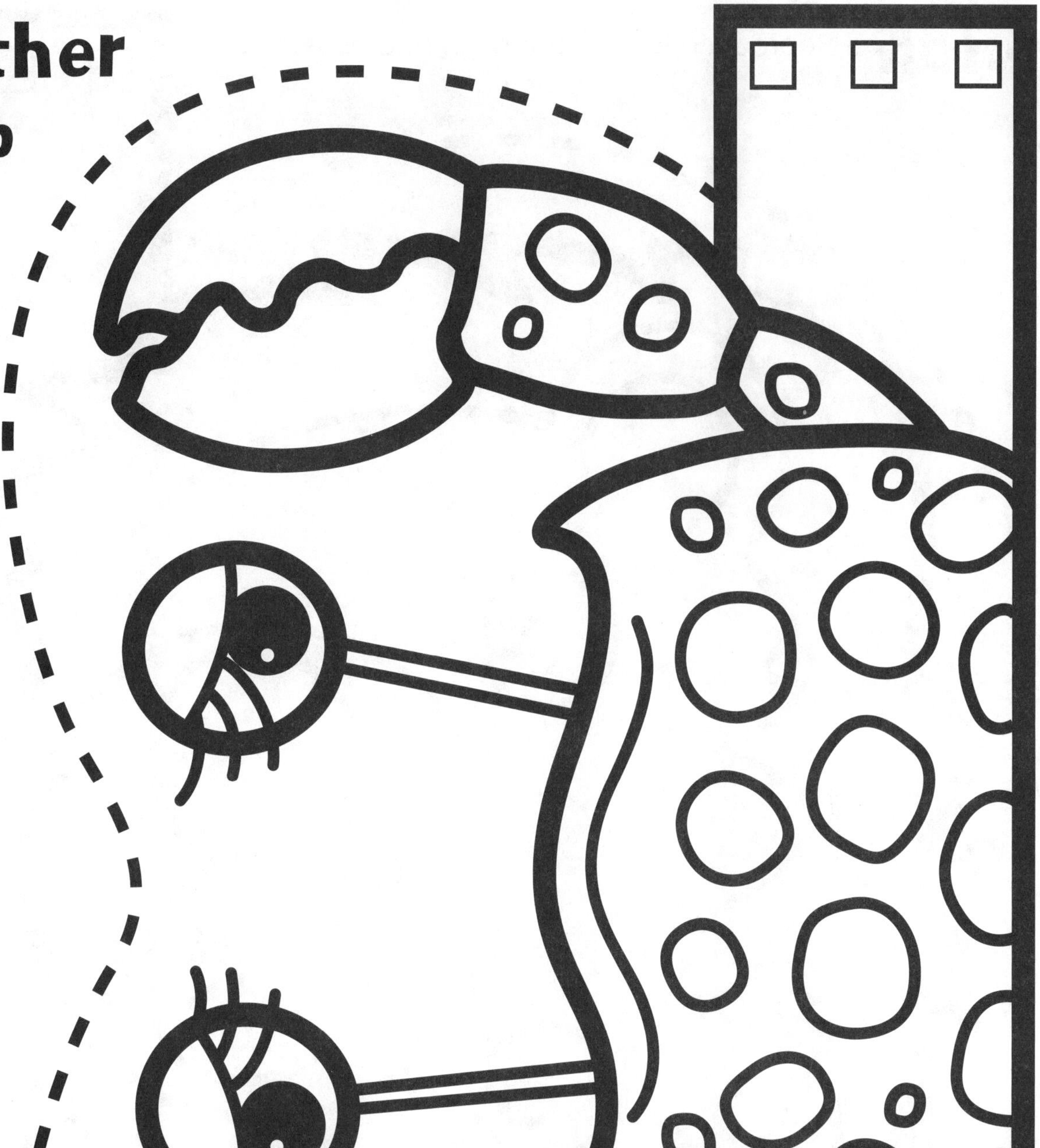

Lion

Reproduce, color, cut, align and assemble

Mouse

Reproduce, color, cut, align and assemble

Chick

Reproduce, color, cut, align and assemble

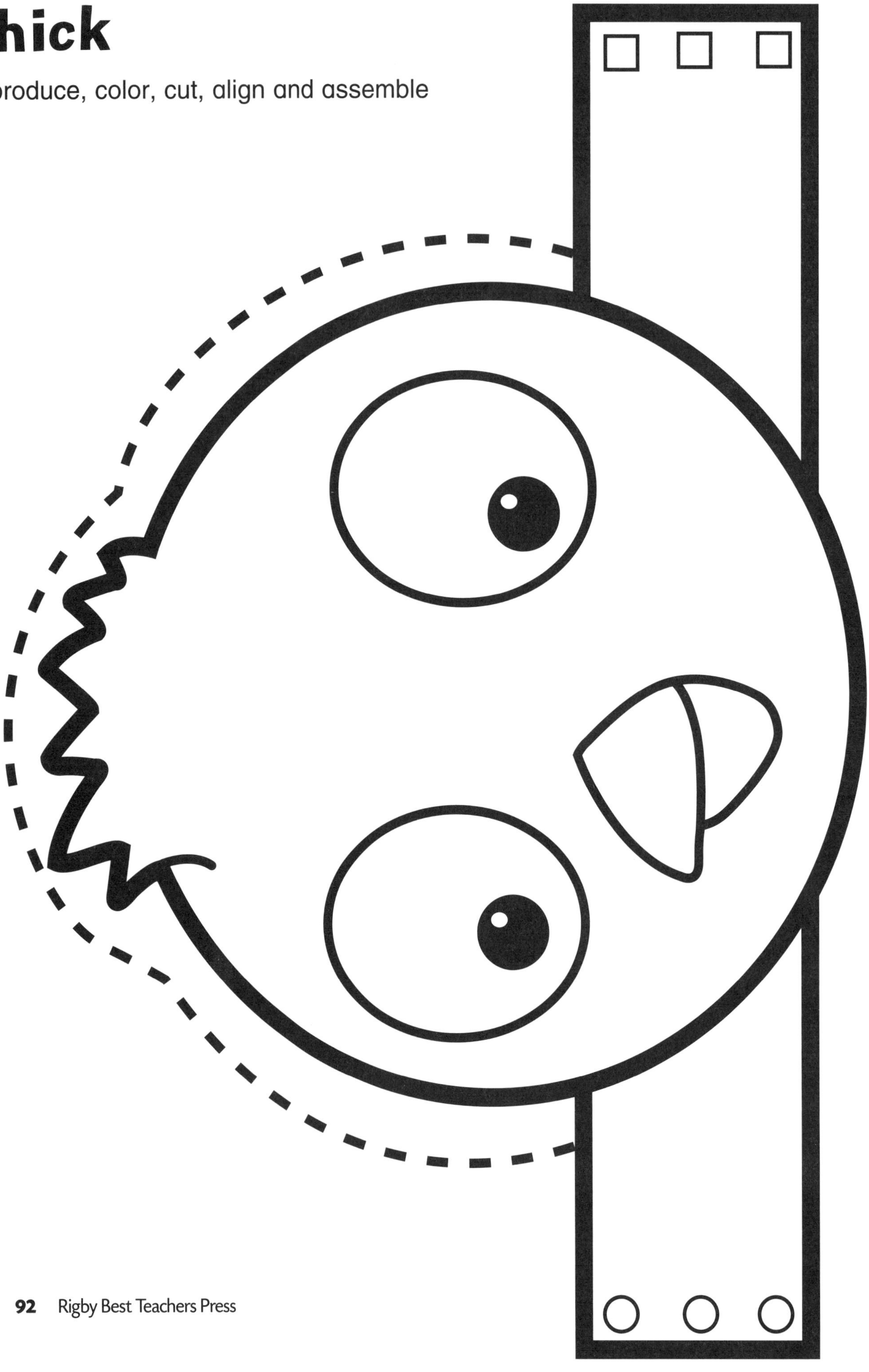

Pig

Reproduce, color, cut, align and assemble

Horse

Reproduce, color, cut, align and assemble

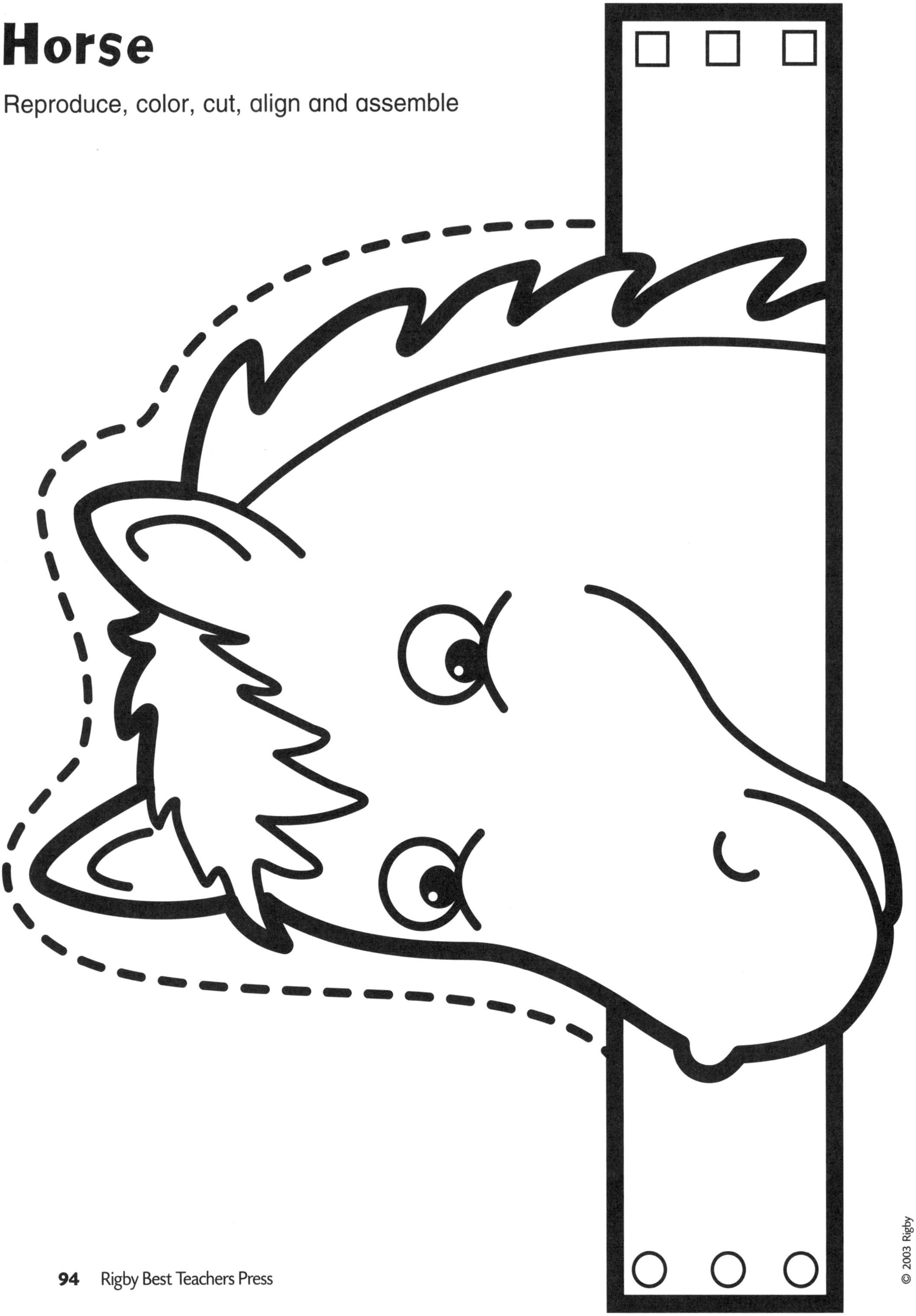

Cow's Tail

Reproduce, color, cut, align and assemble

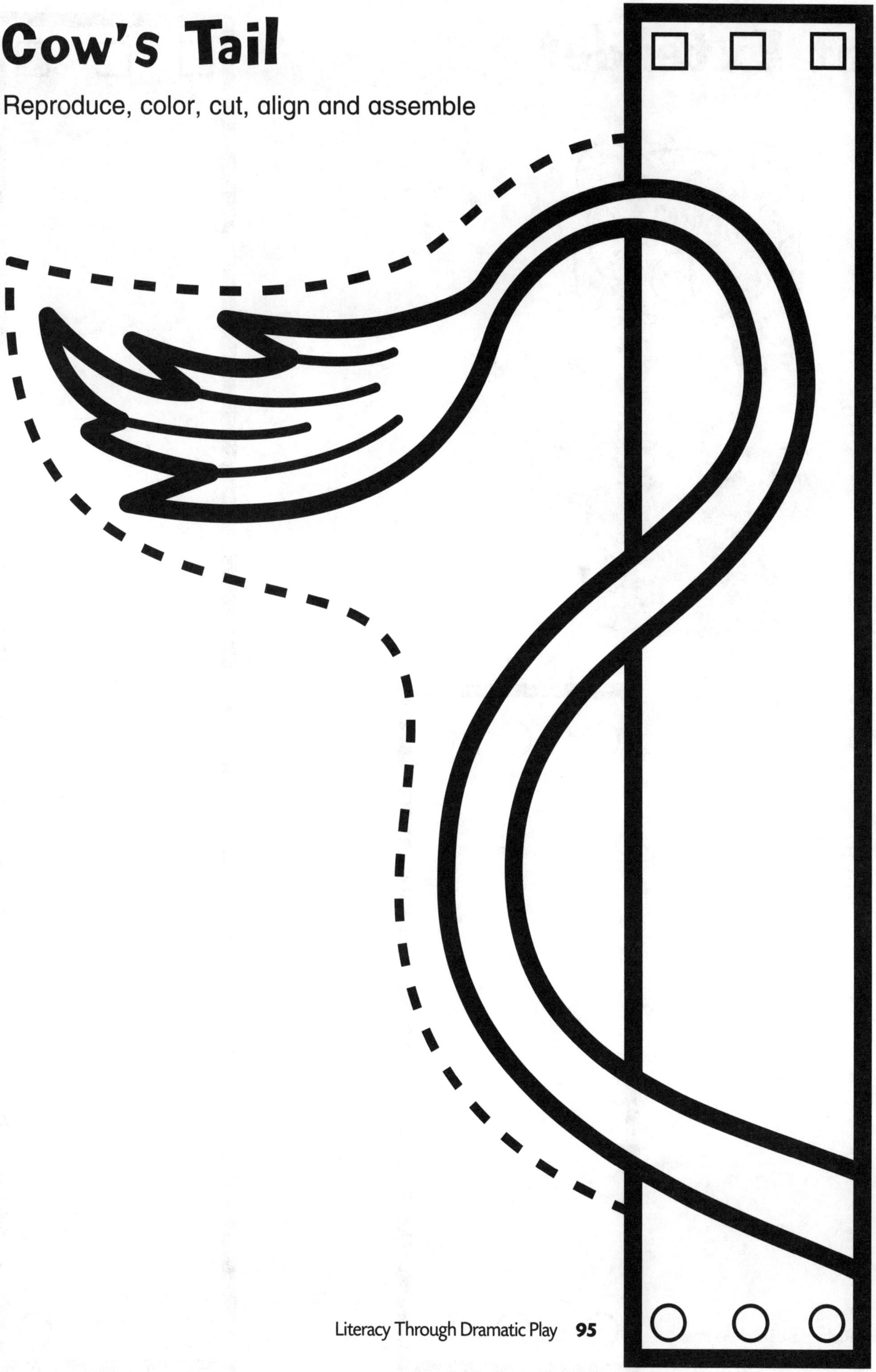

Hat Extender